Praise for Mike James:

"Throughout *Journeyman's Suitcase* Mike James calls the question with regard to how we look at the world and what we see. In "Saint Heresy in the Garden" the poet tells us *It's not always enough to believe in darkness or the simple brokenhearted. / So I believe in Bigfoot, jackalopes, and Mother Mary illuminated on burnt toast.* It's like he's whispering in the most inclusive tone. Then, in "Fallen Angel," we are gifted the backstory of all outliers: *The first job he took, after he quit Heaven, was at a butcher shop. His halo sliced meat pretty well. The shop owner liked the novelty, as did customers used to nothing more interesting than sausage plumpness*; while in "Ed the Entrepreneur" we hear: *Really, life was a game of tag where he was never it. So he spoke like the bumper stickers he loved to read.* We should be grateful for those who show us what being one of the seven point seven billion souls on this planet is about: *Like good cowboys we practice our gallop on broomsticks. If we don't get splinters, we call it a good day.* Mike James says *The best map would reflect stars* and I believe this mapmaker because, in poem after poem, he follows his own best advice and includes the stars."

—Roy Bentley, *Walking with Eve in the Loved City*
(selected by Billy Collins as a finalist for
the 2018 Miller Williams Poetry Prize)

"*Journeyman's Suitcase* is an absurdist, heretical romp; Mike James, through his ability to turn a phrase, to make each poem spark with insight or humor (often both), is our guide, assuring us that *it's not always enough to believe in darkness or in the simple broken-hearted.* This collection is peopled with characters charming and strange: one keeps *a miniature Phoenix as a pet, just to light cigars,* while another has a smile with *the look of a bird's nest with no eggs.* Throughout these poems, James reveals the slipperiness of self, of certainty: *My shadow's always been luckier than me,* he writes, reminding us we are all fallen angels and wayward saints—and that we can find ourselves, and our shadows, in these poems."

—Amie Whittemore, author of *Glass Harvest*

Journeyman's Suitcase

Poems by Mike James

Luchador Press
Big Tuna, TX

Copyright (c) Mike James, 2020
First Edition 1 3 5 7 9 10 8 6 4 2
ISBN: 978-1-950380-86-2
LCCN: 2020930904

Design, edits and layout: El Dopa
Author photo: Molly James
All rights reserved. No part of this publication may be reproduced or transmitted in any form or by any means, electronic or mechanical, including photocopying, recording or by info retrieval system, without prior written permission from the author.

Some of these poems, in current or previous versions, appeared in the following magazines: *As It Ought To Be Magazine, Trailer Park Quarterly, Rusty Truck, Vox Populi, Cultural Weekly, Main Street Rag, Street Legal, Unbroken, Post Poems, Gargoyle, Ekphrastic Review, Praxis, Cajun Mutt, Chiron Review, River City,* and *I-70 Review.*

TABLE OF CONTENTS

I.

Follow the Ground, Not the Sky / 1

Saint Heresy in the Garden / 2

False Confessions / 3

Chris's Stigmata of Everyday Choices / 4

Fallen Angel / 5

Pastel Adjustments / 6

Along this Way, Without Red Shoes / 7

Steve's in Thailand, so He Claims / 8

Edgar's Not So Secret Life / 9

Campbell's Soups / 10

Erased de Kooning / 11

Less Than Umpteen Things / 12

My Father's Advice / 13

Ed the Entrepreneur / 14

Uses for Piggy Banks / 15

Armchair Landscapes without Bubble Bath / 16

Quill Island / 17

A Good Day / 18

Inkwell / 19

Those Pearls in My Mouth / 20

She Could Have Been a Seller of Indulgences / 21

II.

How Was Your Walk? / 25

Rinse and Repeat / 26

Landscapes along the Way / 27

Erica Jong Famous / 28

Red Star Beauty Supply / 29

Tattoo Secrets / 30

Desire Buffet / 31

Safe Words / 32

Postscript to a Goodbye / 33

Unfinished Poem / 34

How We Smile / 35

Poem / 36

Lucky / 37

Windshield / 38

Too Far / 39

July Snow Corn / 40

Player Piano / 41

Nostalgia / 42

Clotheslines / 43

Tiny Tim & Bob Dylan in the East Village / 44

Jerzy Kosinski Sends His Regards / 45

Little Hymn in One Part / 46

Frank Sinatra Jr. is Dead / 47

Don Never Married, Despite Adventures / 48

More Charleston, Less Lament / 49

Little Pink Ode with Smiley Face / 50

Test Pattern Minuet / 51

The Fearful Polymath / 52

I.

Follow the Ground, Not the Sky

If I know where I'm going, I don't get there faster. My pace
   doesn't change.
I'm slow, unsteady. I can follow the sun, like on a mission, and
   still lose my way.

My past makes a trail I circle back to. Often, I meet an old self.
   Normally,
Look away. My satchel, stuffed with unsaid things, gets heavier
   and heavier.

Thunderstorms tell me the Devil is real. Lightening reminds me
   to shut
My eyes. Sometimes, I count or hold my breath. Sometimes, I
   play pretend.

I never gave the Devil up. He's always around the next corner or
   ready
To steal my shadow if I turn away. He carries the long list of my
   fears.

In a way, the Devil is my oldest friend. If that sounds sad, it is.
   There's
Never been an angel on my shoulder. Not once. And my
   shoulders are thin.

Saint Heresy in the Garden

Little comes to me as quickly as I wish. There's always that.
I treat my hang ups, phobias, and failings as my most vital parts.

One habit is calling everyone Mary if I like them well enough.
In that case, the name is a gift. Some respond by giving back a quiz.

Some friends part from me. Maybe tired from my latest hobby.
    (AKA obsession.)
Maybe exhausted from certain ticks…my propensity to use a
    ball cap to catch rain.

Any wisdom I have comes from looking, on an almost monthly
    basis, at
Gas station calendars, black-and-white movies, and discarded
    Beatle lyrics.

It's not always enough to believe in darkness or the simple
    broken-hearted.
So I believe in Bigfoot, jackalopes, and Mother Mary
    illuminated on burnt toast.

False Confessions

The time you panhandled for tattoos. The monthly payments
for transcendence. All the famous people either waived at or
had orgies with. The time you found the burnt wreckage of
flaming shoes. Childhood spent tossing pennies behind the
Red Dirt Cabaret. The mother who worked as both a nun and
a stripper. The medical journal contribution about aspirin as a
cure for love sick penguins. How you were the first to capitalize
and conjugate KAPOW. That ability to translate any fairy
language into Yiddish. The parakeets which sang duets while
you scrambled and re-scrambled the eggs from the plain white
chickens you raised. The prize-winning rooster from Borneo.

Chris's Stigmata of Everyday Choices

No matter how old he got, his wants were for things which hurt. He told time by cigarette coughs. All the door-to-door clock sales people knew to skip his house. To make extra certain, Little Bo Peep was his go-to disguise. Now and then, this was back when those things mattered, the night got really dark. Stars were never his friends, not in the sky or in his imaginary drive-in. His smile had the look of a bird's nest with no eggs. Awkward was what he knew, especially when he travelled across the plains and worried about getting lost among tall grass and towns which advertised the resting places of gunfighters and taxidermists. Little Bo Peep was his go-to disguise. Some weekends he climbed a tree and smiled and waited for a bird, any bird, to land. Bird have their own problems we won't discuss here. Most are limited in the ways they can hide.

Fallen Angel

The first job he took, after he quit Heaven, was at a butcher shop. His halo sliced meat pretty well. The shop owner liked the novelty, as did customers used to nothing more interesting than sausage plumpness. But, like even the best Broadway performance, the gig ended. The health department sent him out the door, amid the owner's sobs and sighs. Halos are hard to clean, no matter how strong the disinfectant. Slicing with one violates regulations which date back before phone book popularity.

After the butcher shop, he became a cowboy. He tied a rope to his halo and called it a lasso. It worked almost as well as Wonder Woman's golden lasso. Though she was from a different place.

Pastel Adjustments

His life, a vending machine filled only with Zagnuts. He
was tired of sameness. What he really wanted was a faux
leather knapsack of absurdities. Not for any commonly
misspelled tattoos or a not so lackadaisical snowflake. More
an unhatched egg flying in perfect geometry across the sky
or even wind blowing both ways at once. He had a fondness
for anything not seen. He didn't always drive through ghosts
on his way to work. Though on any morning he might recall
the red of Sally Hedgepath's nail polish. Anything long
remembered becomes something else. As a kid, he liked to
juggle. His mother told him stop that, go outside and hit
a ball. And so he ran and ran like Dick and Jane and Spot.
He learned to speak in simple sentences. All his socks were
black. When he found a penny he picked it up. When he had
enough pennies he rolled them. He never put a red or pink
ribbon on his penny rolls before he took them to the bank,
but he thought about it more than a few times.

Along this Way, without Red Shoes

My hands get sweaty when staring at any door marked
CONFUSION. Also, I get giddy from sugar or an
unexpectedly granted wish. If I read directions, I might
make right choices. As it is, I don't even believe my
horoscope. Scorpio is not in alignment with Saturn beneath
Kentucky's blue moon. I'm willing to grab any doorknob
if I can hold on long enough. If there's a front porch, I
feel like I'm falling. I dream about a mountaintop toss
sometimes. Most days I have the urge to walk backwards.
The world is the same that way, but not the order.

Steve's in Thailand, So He Claims

It's really impolite to smoke in a rickshaw so he eats peanuts
instead and has that Vogue daydream about red flare pants.
The daydream's been in reruns so long he knows every runway
turn. Still, like the ride, it goes on. He knows what he likes and
doesn't mind. Yesterday was more fun than today even if one
or two old scars blossomed red, raw again. Some gardens grow
no matter how little we tend. The traffic immense and almost
post card framed. The driver declines a peanut offer. His
manners, professional and intense. The peanuts are unsalted,
so there's that.

Edgar's Not-So-Secret Life

His clothes all snowmen's discards, so he dressed in
permanent winter. His wind-up clock stayed stuck at one.
That was fine since he didn't believe in a.m. or p.m. or
Mountain Time or that it could rain in Memphis when it
was perfectly sunny here. When he wasn't making a meal of
instant pablum, he liked to tinker with an antique clown car.
One with imaginary horn and time travel switch. And there
were bongo lessons for anyone who asked. All he asked was
the gift of a penny serenade. Remember those? Each song
starts with Ah, ends with Oh well. The best part, Twinkie-
like, in the middle. As for Twinkies, he was fond of them and
found very little to disappoint. In fact, after he gave up coffee,
he remained fond of heavy cream.

Campbell's Soups

The labels have fallen off my soup cans. I'll have a grilled cheese with something for dinner. That's been my day. A morning unicycle ride to the grocery store and the weekly discussion, with myself, about Elizabeth Bishop (pro and con) over a lunch bagel. An afternoon penny toss in front of the courthouse was my favorite social time. I just wish I'd found someone to play with. Penny toss solitaire is less fun. But that's been my day. I followed a cat up a tree. I got stuck. The cat got down. Firemen came and laughed at my kilt and suspenders. I've never met a fireman interested in either fashion or Scottish history. My chief rescuer had tomato soup breath as he carried me down.

Erased de Kooning

after Rauschenberg

Goodbye charcoal. Goodbye ink. Goodbye curious visitors.
Goodbye crayons numbering more than 48 and less than 64.
Goodbye Dutch mumbling. Goodbye pencils 1 and 2 and 7.
Goodbye gestures, grand and hidden. Goodbye New York City
Harbor in daylight, but mainly at night. Goodbye tics, not
quite hidden. Goodbye 61 consecutive work days. Goodbye
hang ups. Goodbye eraser crumbs. Don't sneeze. Or do.
Goodbye woman as wife and subject. Goodbye women and
women. Hello traces. Hello shadows large and medium size
and small. Hello hints, almost too subtle. Wave like the queen
when you wave. Lots and lots of hellos.

Less Than Umpteen Things

I'm going to go out and join a fight club as soon as I leave the nail salon. By that, of course, I mean I am going to the cat rescue center and do my Sunday shopping. This morning started off badly when the sun rose in the north and not even the local rooster knew what to do. At some point, Chicken Little will be proved right. I try to reference Chicken Little at least once a week. Normally, that reference comes on a Tuesday. That's what's on my calendar anyway. I really loved false positive narratives as a child. These days I love crossword puzzles and action movies, a little bourbon in my Shirley Temple and a spell check on my home tattoo kit. We all have to give up things after a while. I'm going to give up sunglasses as soon as this pair wears out.

My Father's Advice

If you find yourself in a black and white movie, watch out
for quicksand. That's not something you hear every day,
but by that point he was already dreaming about kudzu on
the fence's other side. Mother already gone off to the always
discount store. No one else to tell me where to go, what to do,
the best way to make grill cheese without cheese or bread,
or the seven best names for a pet fish. A parent's work, never
done. All I learned on my own came from the time I invited
a dung beetle to my birthday party. That kindness never
repeated. Both my parents, all the guests, said rightfully,
never again.

Ed the Entrepreneur

He thought he could make more money selling acoustic
versions of his formal poems. He did better selling
nostalgia cookies in the past tense. Really, life was a game
of tag where he was never it. So he spoke like the bumper
stickers he loved to read. He even put up flyers advertising
his claw foot bathtub souvenirs. They were featured at
the local leather shop. On Thursday's (he was a Thursday
person), he stopped in the shop and told jokes to the owner.
The owner loved knock-knock jokes. He did too. He really
loved ones were no one answered. His doorbell hadn't
worked for years.

Uses for Piggy Banks

When they are not pink they still seem to think pink
thoughts. Projection doesn't make that less true. There's no
practical use for pink like there is for money. Think pink
house in a yellow field, no tree or neighbor in sight. Farmers
are practical and must be. Maybe this one loves pigs and
flamingos.

Money is a kind of poetry, Wally said. And that doesn't
rhyme, the young girl replied. Change rhymes with game or
nearly so.

The empty pig makes no sound. Then there's the rattle of
coins sliding in. One by one. Large and small. Small and
small. The child makes a game of this. She chants a nonsense
rhyme with the rattle. She never names the game.

Archaic Landscape without Bubble Bath

Whenever he had bad dreams, he realized he had watched
the news. Stuffed animals, graham crackers, plastic water
bottles, and baby dolls were all in cages. The cage wire looked
like sand paper. Desert sand speckled the wire throughout
night and day. So at least sand and wind still worked together.
The stuffed animals held the most color. The air was dry
and dryer. And, of course, the sky lacked rain. So nothing
bloomed on plains or hills. The clouds went west or south or
stayed in the north. After a while no one thought to look at
the sky.

Quill Island

There are mermaids here, the same as in Thailand. Which seems appropriate since a sailor's shanty is the local fight song. If you are looking for trouble, they have every desire which starts with z. Palm readers blush over expletives when they share good news and hand care advice. An exactly noon parade reminds every one of the time and to eat lunch and that they are not in New Orleans or Kansas. Lunch coupons are a popular currency. If you forget to bring some, street vendors can supply you in exchange for your shoes.

A Good Day

That game where we pretend to be strangers and get married anyway. I think it's called Paradox Heaven. Normally, it ends in a draw. Most days, we try to be angels though it's hard not to curse in our prayers. Neither of us has a pedigree longer than a postage stamp. Family history is mainly a secret no one wants to share. On days when we don't shoot stop signs we like to research circuses to run away to. Elephant riding is something we might enjoy. Like good cowboys we practice our gallop on broomsticks. If we don't get splinters, we call it a good day.

Inkwell

More modern than the abacus, but less often used. An
antique for bright hatted eccentrics buried beneath peacock
colored scarves. The perfect gift for the neighbor who wears
a monocle.

Victor is my monocle wearing neighbor. Behind his back
everyone calls him, that monocle guy. Since culture for him
is the heaviest of heavy creams, he doesn't have many friends.
At the neighborhood cookouts he handles the drunks and
the insomniacs. He's very good with animals. You can see
him in his backyard, standing like St. Francis, with birds up
and down his arms.

Those Pearls in My Mouth

I wish I had a better smile. That sounds like a paid
endorsement for a dentistry chain, but it's not quite. I laugh
behind my hands as if I'm holding my secrets in. No one's
ever told me if that works. After I laugh I should always
ask whoever I'm with what they know about me. If they
look confused, I'll know my hands are doing their job. That
might give me confidence in my hand's ability to do other,
more magical things. I might even let them try to snap out a
rhythm, while I hum along with flight dreams.

She Could Have Been a Seller of Indulgences

It was never easy for her especially on Tuesday, as we know
how Tuesdays are with those leftover promises from the start
of the week and the day before. It's probably not enough
that every third day she wore a sun dress to keep the sun
interested and nearby.

Or that she kept a miniature Phoenix as a pet, just to light
her cigars. That wasn't her only pet, but the one people
mentioned. They also talked about how she rubbed her
ring-covered fingers together when she listened. She mainly
did that on Wednesday when she held dining room court.
Mainly and only might have been her favorite words and
might have been most descriptive of her, as might have
been was her favorite phrase. Everyone, from the queen to
nail technicians, loved her dinners of dry chardonnay and
saltines.

II

How Was Your Walk?

It rained on one side of the street, but not the other.
Sundays in August are like that.
I got all wet on the sidewalk.
My shadow stayed dry on the road.
Neither of us carry an umbrella.
Neither of us ever tries to outrun the rain in lonesome
    tap shoes.
My shadow's always been luckier than me.
Lots of people say that, but for me it's true.
On the other side of the street are wild daisies.
I never pick them.
I always worry and worry about ticks and snakes.
My dry shadow touched each one.

Rinse and Repeat

after Catullus

I hate.
I love.
Of course, I fuck…or try to.
Is that enough to complete any season?
Throw pain in the middle.
A little recipe for want.
Against judgement.
Yep. Against reason.

Landscapes along the Way

I can't identify any flowers.
Gertrude Stein would be so ashamed.
My great-grandmother was quite the gardener.
She died before I was born, but people said she was quite
    the gardener.
Most of those people are dead too.
I don't think there are any court papers about her
    gardening.
Maybe some crusty newspaper clippings.
Small town newspapers like that sort of thing.
I haven't looked.
I'm lazy and I think I have allergies.
I haven't checked with a doctor or a nurse or a neighbor.
I just weep a lot in sunshine.
I weep a lot on dark nights too.
Sometimes, I sneeze after weeping.
I'm always surrounded by flowers.

Erica Jong Famous

Erica Jong was a poet famous in the 1970's.
I was born in the 1970's.
She loved to write about sex.
Critics called her the "female Henry Miller."
I like sex and I've read a lot of Henry Miller.
I guess that means I either like Henry Miller or want to
     sound educated about
Henry Miller things.
I don't think a Henry Miller quote ever seduced anyone.
I don't think an Erica Jong quote ever seduced anyone.
Whenever I say her name I worry I'm mispronouncing it.
I worry about mispronouncing a lot of things.
My accent is super southern.
Tennessee Williams could be my uncle if I believed in uncles.
I don't think Tennessee Williams would believe in me.
No one has every corrected my pronunciation of Erica Jong.
That could change on a city sidewalk tomorrow.
Erica Jong's first book is called Fruits & Vegetables.
That title is easy to remember.
It makes me hungry and makes me giggle.

Red Star Beauty Supply

I told her I wanted smoky eyes.
She lit a cigar.
I told her I wanted a makeover.
She suggested mud pies.
I told her I wasn't happy with my looks.
She took away my mirror.

I hang out there a lot.
One day I hope she'll hire me, as cashier.

Tattoo Secrets

My tattoos help me remember my secrets.
Thankfully, my tattoo artist is also an Egyptologist.
If that sounds like a rare combo, it is.
Sometimes, we have coffee together.
We don't talk much.
His great love is hieroglyphics.
He draws a sun or a snake or a foot on a napkin.
I try and guess what his meaning is.

Desire Buffet

Give up boundaries for your hunger.
Taste, luxuriate in the mess of juices.
Then go on.
Eat your utensils.
Your napkin.
Munch away at your plate and cup.
Finish with a few nibbles on the table and chair.

Safe Words

Orange peel.
Twisted duck.
Asparagus.
Road work.
Shivering kabobs.
Lucky Luciano.
Home grown disco.

Postscript to a Goodbye

Let me go and let me be gone and stay there.

Unfinished Poem

for Larry Levis

Here are desires, cave deep.

Here is the man and woman who kiss secrets on your bed,

while every light burns in the house.

Here is the dream of the butterfly tattoo and the red shoe box

    of letters.

Here is dust shaken off as an offering on your doorstep.

Here is part of the river you always carry.

Here is one piece to a child's puzzle.

The puzzle piece resembles a mountain or an ocean seen far off.

Here is the sound of skipping rope.

Here are dandelions, fresh from the ditch's edge.

How We Smile

The corners of our lips start a fight with gravity.
The fight doesn't last long.
Gravity wins, oh, gravity wins.
Our tongues stay hidden, plotting.

Poem

Talking to him was like talking to a mirror.
Talking to him was like talking to yourself.
I love talking to myself.
I love talking to mirrors.
It's great when there's a mirror smile.
Lots of time that has to do with good hair.

Lucky

The nickname, a harsh joke.
His bad luck was all he counted on.
Like red dirt it stuck to everything.

Windshield

So there you go, he said.
Meaning?
Almost anything.
The conversation continued, racetrack quick.
His personality driving, driving.

Too Far

A map keeps you from too far.
That's a map's job.

The best map would reflect stars.

July Snow Corn

If heat made all the corn in the field pop open
Popcorn would be so high
An airplane pilot would think it was snow.

Player Piano

The player piano is winding down.
No one at the bar can fix it.
There's not a phone number for anyone to call.
Every song is like mice walking slowly across tin.

We still gather around the piano to stomp our feet.
Frank and Libby sing duets like always.
Frank still mispronounces most words.
Libby is loud enough no one notices.

Nostalgia

Spoon fresh taste of apple jelly right from the jar

Clotheslines

for Ed Smith

This is the borderline.
This is crossing the line.

This is a fishing line.
These are poetry lines.

None are really long lines.
Even the fishing line.

Set aside the bad lines.
Cultivate pickup lines.

Build a house on the line.
Decorate with clothesline.

Tiny Tim & Bob Dylan in the East Village

Tiny Tim is both stage name and misnomer. He's 6'1, but
the crouch in his walk makes him look stouter, shorter.
He and the kid from Minnesota share oily fries for lunch.
Both are as unknown as the man sleeping on the bench
outside the bar. They pay with change that isn't spare. Only
drink water.

Dylan makes up stories about being a runaway and a circus
clown, about a neighborhood widow he loved and left in
scandal. Tiny listens and listens, but doesn't believe. He'd
tell about vaudeville if he was there or could imagine. He'd
like another order of fries or some woman to love him
badly. He'd like an extra set of strings for his ukulele. He'd
like ketchup with the fries. Dylan hates ketchup.

Jerzy Kosinski Sends His Regards

Fiction and the afterlife have much in common. Both are made up of people we wish we met and people we wish we hadn't. Elvis occupies both spheres. Saying that is not nice, but it's true and truth has its own scrappy virtue. The last part is a maxim. The dead speak in those. There are almost as many clichés as there is time to fill.

Little Hymn in One Part

Andy goes weekend dumpster diving. Neither of us know what he's lost. He ignores the food, but takes out cat scratched stools and cracked lumber. Once, he found a perfectly good leather dog leash re-used to wrangle passing clouds. Oddly, he's not a believer in daytime rain or in the way Rome fell as explained by Gibbon. As you'd expect, he loves gas stations for the smell of the hot dogs they serve. His preferred fork was found while smoking at a gas bump. He will do a pirouette at any gas station where customers are generous with change. He only levitates when he feels like showing off. You wouldn't guess he's a gigolo and street mime, sometimes dressed as an angel. He lives off cotton candy and French fries. No one has ever seen him eat a hot dog.

Frank Sinatra Jr. is Dead

Yawning over obituaries is only fine if no one else is around.
A fact left out of charm school. Most people who fail charm
school go by anonymous. Though some go into politics
or the ministry. I met one charm school dropout who
became a model, but didn't last long. She kept forgetting
those wide-eyed turns. Also, it was boring. She said so and
such bluntness carries its own charm. One day she skipped
work because it was raining. It hadn't rained all summer.
She spent the day walking, looking at the rain, and saying,
Where have you been?

Don Never Married, Despite Adventures

Barely a teenager when he discovered scratch and sniff pornography, he quickly found other interests. Weekends were spent observing bovine tomfoolery. That led to unlicensed canoe rides to taunt paddleboat honeymooners. After a while, he bought a telephone shaped like Van Gogh's ear and spent an hour each day calling radio stations to share quotes from Oliver Cromwell and Marcel Marceau. All his friends were papier-mache puppets held together by sweaty glue and aspirational glitter. An insomniac, he obsessed over the secular problems of the afterlife. Every third sidewalk stranger found him beautiful. Of course, it was his hair. Thick red, it burned half-way down his back. Everyone mentioned it. It's stunning what people overlook, even on a penny laden sidewalk.

More Charleston, Less Lament

Those voices in your head sound like 1920's musicals. When they sound like something else you change the tune to another time you never knew. It wasn't always like this. As a child you loved bird songs more than chiffon and you loved chiffon more than chocolate and you loved chocolate more than you loved most relatives, almost all strangers. To hear birds better you'd find out what all the neighbors were doing, then go to a tree far away. In the summer, the trees were towns without mail. In the winter, you watched the sky from indoors. The voices told you how to climb any summer tree, never how to get down.

Little Pink Ode with Smiley Face

It was about the time I was old enough to vote, drink,
and play subway guitar without embarrassment. Newly
degreed in dust bunny analysis, I was already good at faking
sincerity. For all the common reasons, I was stepping away
from real estate and into role playing. Usually, I was a large
bunny with a bleach and sugarcane problem. Every surprise
I came upon was a little vacation. Most days were spent not
being fancy, just being dancy. When I went to get mail I
always tried to impersonate John Wayne's walk. None of my
neighbors knew John Wayne. They thought of me as the red
bathrobe man who always carried a pinwheel.

Test Pattern Minuet

He liked large, gray rubber bands. We all have our interests.
Not that he had much of a collection. And the ones he had
were all large and gray. So much for variety. Sometimes he
would spin a rubber band around and around on one of his
long index fingers while he hummed and thought of green.
He almost always thought of green when he hummed,
regardless the tune. This had nothing to do with his tarot
cards or his daily horoscope reads. Often, it rained right
after he finished humming. He almost never thought of
flowers.

The Fearful Polymath

The thought of rising tides and no boats is one fear.
Mismatched socks, another. Do you often run naked right
out of your dreams? Don't worry, at least you aren't falling
into a constellation of hair which has never approached
a brush. None of that is on today's calendar, in red ink or
otherwise. Though, right on time, the man in the Sunday
croquet outfit comes along. He's selling snow cones/advice
combos. No matter what you get, the price is the same. So
you go with a cherry/blueberry mix and normal, gypsy
clichés. He adds a tiny umbrella so you look more like an
adult while you lick and crunch your ice.

Mike James makes his home outside Nashville, Tennessee. He has published in numerous magazines throughout the country in such places as *Plainsongs, Laurel Poetry Review, Birmingham Poetry Review,* and *Chiron Review.* His poetry collections include: *Parades* (Alien Buddha), *Jumping Drawbridges in Technicolor* (Blue Horse), *First-Hand Accounts from Made-Up Places* (Stubborn Mule), *Crows in the Jukebox* (Bottom Dog), *My Favorite Houseguest* (FutureCycle), and *Peddler's Blues* (Main Street Rag.) He served as an associate editor of *The Kentucky Review* and currently serves as an associate editor of *Unbroken.*